MAKO SHARKS

Anne Welsbacher

Capstone Press

M I N N E A P O L I S

Capstone Press • 2440 Fernbrook Lane • Minneapolis, MN 55447

Editorial Director   John Coughlan
Managing Editor   John Martin
Production Editor   James Stapleton
Copy Editor   Thomas Streissguth

Library of Congress Cataloging-in-Publication Data

Welsbacher, Anne, 1955-
  Mako sharks / by Anne Welsbacher.
    p. cm. -- (Sharks)
    Includes bibliographical references (p.) and index.
    ISBN 1-56065-272-1
    1. Shortfin mako--Juvenile literature. 2. Mako sharks--
Juvenile literature. [1. Mako sharks. 2. Sharks.] I. Title. II.
Series: Welsbacher, Anne, 1955-   Sharks.
  QL638.95.L3W44 1996
  597'.31--dc20   95-7351
                                                                CIP
                                                                 AC

Table of Contents

Range Map.. 4

Facts about Mako Sharks 5

Chapter 1 Built for Speed.............................. 7

Chapter 2 The Mako Eating Machine 19

Chapter 3 The Life of a Mako 29

Chapter 4 Attack! Fighting for Their Lives.. 35

Glossary 43

To Learn More 45

About the Author... 46

Index 47

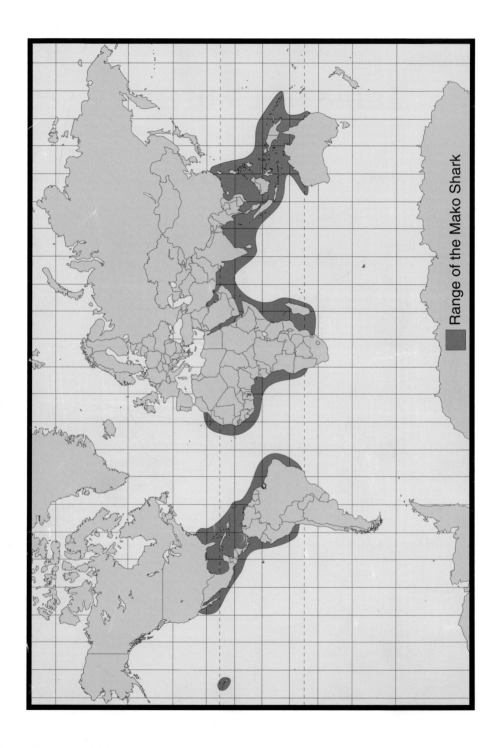

Range of the Mako Shark

Facts about Mako Sharks

Scientific name: *Isurus oxyrinchus*

Common names: Mako, shortfin mako, sharp-nosed mackerel shark. In Australia, it's called the blue pointer.

Closest relatives: Longfin mako, great white shark, and porbeagle.

Description: A streamlined shark with sharply pointed snout, dark eyes, slender body, large teeth, and small back fin.

Length: Makos reach 12 feet (3.6 meters). Average length is about 6.5 feet (2 meters).

Weight: Makos weigh up to 1,000 pounds (453 kilograms); the largest weigh as much as 1,300-plus pounds (591 kilograms).

Color: Dark metallic blue above and white below.

Food: Fish and squid.

Location: Makos swim in the warm and temperate (nearly warm) oceans of the world.

Chapter 1

Built for Speed

It's a furious fighter. It will jump high into the air. It will jump right into a boat. It will even attack a boat.

It's built to move fast. It has been clocked at 60 miles (97 kilometers) an hour.

It has teeth like daggers, teeth that can tear apart the biggest prey.

It's the mako, the fastest, meanest-looking shark in the world.

Fast in the Water

Makos are built like good airplanes. They are **streamlined** so the water does not drag on

Isurus oxyrinchus glides near the surface, looking for prey.

them. They have cone-shaped snouts that come to a sharp point. The snout cuts easily through the water. Their powerful tails give them a lot of thrust, like a jet engine.

A mako moves fast when it is chasing prey or trying to break free from a fishing hook.

Makos have been clocked at 60 miles (97 kilometers) per hour. But their usual chasing speed is about 20 to 35 miles (32 to 56 kilometers) or more per hour.

When the mako is not chasing food or in danger, it cruises at a slow 2 miles (3.2 kilometers) per hour. Most sharks swim less than a mile, or about 1.6 kilometers, an hour.

At that pace, makos can keep on swimming for a long time. One mako traveled 36 miles (58 kilometers) a day for 37 days. Another shark swam 1,700 miles (2,700 kilometers) from Virginia in the United States to the West Indies.

Big Blue

Although most makos are about the size of a large human being, makos that live a long time may reach about 10 to 12 feet (3 to 3.7 meters) in length.

Teeth of fossil makos have been found. They show that ancient makos may have weighed two tons and may have measured 20 feet long.

Like many sharks, makos are dark on top and light on the bottom. Their bright metallic-blue backs darken to dark blue when they are out of the water. A band of silver divides the blue from the white underside. A mako's shiny skin is smooth.

The mako and its relatives can be quickly recognized by their tails. Unlike most sharks, their tails are curved, with the parts above and below the body about equal in size and shape. In fact, the mako family's scientific name, *Isuridae,* means "equal tails."

Many sharks have two **dorsal**, or back, fins. The mako has one fairly large one in the middle of the body and a much smaller one back toward the tail.

A Keel for Speed

The mako's streamlined body helps it move fast. Another thing that helps is its **keel**. The keel is a hard, flat part that sticks out from the narrow body just before the tail.

The streamlined body of the mako makes it one of the fastest sharks in the water.

The keel of a boat sticks down into the water from the boat's bottom. The keel of a mako sticks out to the sides, giving it more power. Many strong muscles in the mako's tail are attached to the keel. So it plays an important part in helping the shark to swim fast and powerfully.

Important Gills

Most fish get oxygen through gills instead of through lungs. Mako sharks have five large **gill slits** on the side of the body. Water enters the slits and passes over the thin gills. The gills take oxygen from the water.

A mako's gill slits are extra long, so that the shark can get the extra oxygen its body needs for its bursts of speed.

Their warm bodies also help makos move at top speed. Most fish lose heat from their blood through their gills. Makos and their relatives do not. The heat stays in the body, keeping the muscles ready for action.

Makos are so famous for speed that people who see any fast shark may call it a mako.

Meet the Real Mako

The mako shark belongs to a small group of sharks called mackerel sharks. The famed man-eating great white shark is also a mackerel shark.

Mackerel sharks were probably named for mackerel fish, because both have a keel at the base of the tail. But a mackerel is a bony fish. Its skeleton is made of bones, like a human's.

Sharks, however, have no bones. Instead, they are made up of **cartilage**. Cartilage is softer than bone, but it is still stiff. Humans have cartilage in their noses, ears, and kneecaps.

The mako is also called the sharp-nosed mackerel shark or the shortfin mako. The fin on its side (its **pectoral** fin) is shorter than the one on its closest relative, the longfin mako.

Where They Live

Mako sharks live in all the major oceans of the world. They like warm or almost warm water. They often stay in the region where cold and warm ocean water meet. There are a lot of fish there for them to catch.

For a long time, scientists thought that the mako of the Atlantic Ocean and the mako of the Pacific were different **species**, or kinds, of

Gill slits on the sides of the mako allow the fish to take in oxygen.

shark. Now they know that shortfin makos are the same all over the world.

Makos swim in deep waters. They don't often come close to shore. That is why swimmers don't often see them.

That's a good thing, because makos can be very dangerous!

Chapter 2

The Mako Eating Machine

Powerful makos need a lot of food for energy. These sharks spend most of their lives hunting for food.

Different sharks eat different foods. What they like depends partly on where they live. Makos live out in the open sea. Their bodies and their teeth are made for catching fast fish and other animals.

Makos stay very busy hunting food. They eat many times their own weight every year. Sometimes a mako will swim through a school

The lower teeth of a mako shark look like curved daggers.

of fish with its mouth open, gulping down whole fish as fast as it can.

Growing Up

The things makos eat change as they grow. Smaller makos (up to about 300 pounds, or 136 kilograms) have long, pointed teeth. They use them to catch fish and squid. Mackerel make a nice meal for smaller makos.

As sharks get bigger, their teeth get bigger, too. They become more like knives. A big mako can eat big fish such as swordfish and marlin. They may catch dolphins or seals.

A mako does not chew its food. It usually swallows its prey whole. One time a whole 120-pound (54-kilogram) swordfish was found inside the stomach of a 700-pound (318-kilogram) mako.

Mako Teeth

Most sharks have teeth that angle backward into their mouths when their mouths are closed. But a mako's bottom teeth always stand upright. Its lower teeth look like curved daggers that stick up from its lower jaw. This makes a mako frightening when seen up close.

Many sharks have teeth that are jagged, or **serrated**, like a saw blade, on the sides. A mako's teeth are more like smooth knives. They are not serrated. The knife-like teeth can easily grasp large prey.

Makos have eight rows of teeth in their jaws. The front row is used for eating. When a

Blue on top and silvery on the bottom, the mako disguises itself by blending into the water's changing colors.

shark loses a front tooth, another one moves up from behind to replace it. Sometimes this new tooth, fully grown, moves into place in only 24 hours!

Sharks' teeth are often found on beaches. In New Zealand, the native people often wore mako teeth to decorate their ears.

Fast-Moving Meals

Makos are the fastest sharks. So it's not surprising that they eat fast-moving fish. Makos go after other sharks, tunas, herring, squid, mackerel, bluefish, and swordfish.

Swordfish are big, even as big as a big shark. But that doesn't stop makos from chasing them for a good meal. Makos have

Makos hunt and attack using all six of their senses.

been known to go after swordfish one-third their own size. Makos have been caught with the whole sword from a swordfish hanging off their flesh.

Hearing and Touching

Sharks have ears for hearing sound. But you can't see an outer ear on a shark's head. The hearing organ is hidden away behind the thick skin of the head. It is very sensitive. It can hear sounds much lower in pitch than people can hear.

Sharks also have a special sense that is like both hearing and touch. Running along the side of the shark's body and into its head and inner ear is a strip of sensing cells. This special sensory strip is called the **lateral line**.

The lateral line senses motion in the water. Sharks use the lateral line to become aware of moving fish and other distant motion. They can sense movements that are too small for humans to see.

Seeing the Light

Eyesight is not very important to many sharks. But sharks do see some colors. They like bright colors, like the bright orange used on life vests. Sharks are so attracted to this color that scientists call it "yum-yum yellow."

Mako sharks have mirror-like cells in the back of their eyes. Cats also have this layer of cells. The cells reflect light back, making them glow in only a little light. The special cells help sharks see in the dim light of the ocean.

The Sixth Sense

Sharks have another sense that no other animal has. Tiny pores, or holes, on their heads are filled with a watery fluid. These pores are called **ampullae of Lorenzini**. (An ampoule is a small bottle). The man who discovered them was named Lorenzini.

All living creatures give off tiny electrical signals. The moving muscles of animals give off an especially good signal. Ampullae of Lorenzini can sense these electrical signals from moving fish.

A mako can see, smell, hear, detect motion, and sense electrical signals. This makes them very dangerous hunters.

Wounded prey send out even stronger electrical signals. So sharks zoom in on them. Sometimes sharks have kept attacking the same victim, even if another fish gets closer. Scientists believe this is because of the strong electrical signal the wounded victim is sending out.

Putting the Senses to Work

Sharks use all their senses in hunting.

First, they smell their prey. Often they smell the blood of a wounded, bleeding animal.

In wartime, when ships have exploded, sharks were drawn to the wounded men in the water. Sharks can also "hear" the low sounds of splashing fish (or swimmers).

When a hunting mako gets closer to possible food, vision kicks in. Sharks can tell light from dark and some colors.

But they are more likely to actually locate their prey when the ampullae of Lorenzini start to buzz. Then the shark can pick up the prey's electrical signals. A shark might actually bump into its prey by using this sense.

The shark might then take a bite–but it is still testing. The shark might decide it doesn't want what its senses led it to. It will spit out its catch and swim away.

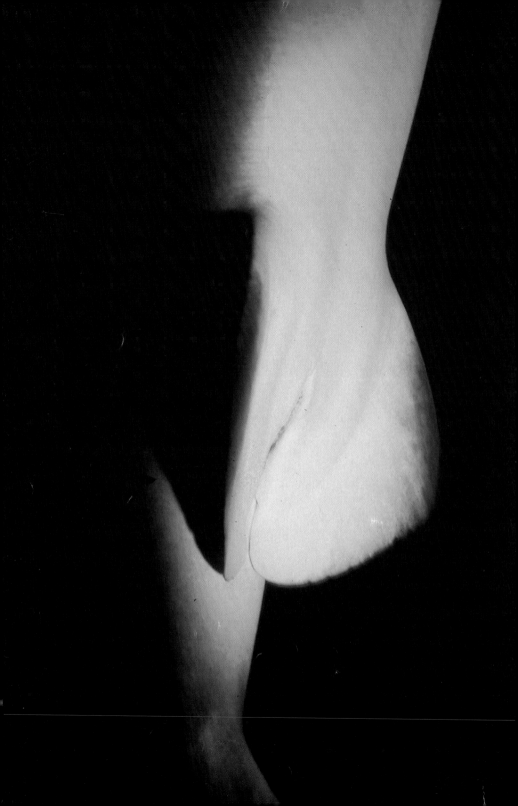

Chapter 3

The Life of a Mako

Young mako sharks grow faster than most other sharks. The pups often grow about a foot each year until they are full grown.

Makos swim the oceans all alone, except when they mate. A male will be ready to mate when it is about 6.5 feet (2 meters) long. A female will be bigger, about 8.5 feet (2.6 meters).

Mating Habits

Most female fish lay eggs, which are fertilized when the male releases sperm over them. But mako eggs are fertilized inside the female.

The female mako lays eggs through the cloaca, between her pelvic fins.

When a male mako happens to find a willing female, he approaches and bumps her. He bites her hard, leaving deep scars.

Male sharks use special organs called **claspers** to mate with females. Claspers look rather like small fins on their abdomens. They are used to hold onto the female.

The male slides one clasper into an opening on the female. Then a channel inside the clasper sends sperm into the female's body, where it fertilizes the eggs.

From Eggs to Young

Mako eggs hatch inside the mother. The hatched young, called pups, continue to grow inside, nice and warm. They eat other eggs that the mother's body keeps producing. In fact, they eat so much that they are born with fat stomachs filled with food. This keeps them going for several days.

The claspers of the male mako are used in mating.

A shark gives birth to its pups along the ocean floor.

When mako pups are about 26 inches (65 centimeters) long, the pups are born. They are born ready to start swimming.

The mako shark usually gives birth to 4 or 5 pups. Most sharks have 6 to 12 pups. But some, like the tiger and hammerhead, have as many as 40.

Out into the World

The pups set off on their own adventures in the oceans of the world. They begin to hunt for food right away. Makos hunt at both dusk and dawn, when their prey might be waking up or tired from the day. The sharks themselves probably never sleep.

Scientists don't know how long makos live. Their average age could range from 5 to 12 years old. Or they might live to be as old as 50 years. They probably die when they've used up all their eight rows of teeth and can no longer eat.

Chapter 4
Attack! Fighting for Their Lives

Makos are legends. They are the most exciting fish a fisherman can go after for sport. Books have been written about the fierce battles these game fish have fought to avoid being caught.

When hooked, makos fight long and hard for their lives. And they are **aggressive**. They are the only big-game fish that can bring real danger to the person fishing.

Scientists haul in a mako shark for further examination.

Makos are a challenge to catch, but they also taste good. Their flesh is the best-tasting of all shark meat. Mako is often served in fine restaurants.

In North America, there is good fishing for makos in the Atlantic Ocean off New York. Fishermen also find them in the Gulf of Mexico off Texas.

But the best mako fishing is near Australia and New Zealand. In fact, the native people of New Zealand, called Maori, gave the shark its name of mako.

Leaping for Freedom

A mako's powerful tail helps it to swim very fast, but it also helps it do something else. The mako can use its tail to make a fantastic

This mako was caught during a fishing tournament.

leap out of the water while trying to get rid of the hook.

A mako has been known to surge out of the sea to a height of 20 feet (6 meters). Some fisherman have claimed that a mako had to leap 30 feet (9 meters) high in order to get over his boat. To do that, the shark must get a running start of at least 22 miles (35 kilometers) per hour.

Once, a man speared a mako in shallow water off the coast of Puerto Rico. The mako swam to deeper water, shook out the spear, and came back to the shore. It jumped right onto the shore at the man's feet. Then it jumped back into the ocean and was gone before anyone could catch it.

Attack

When leaping does not free the shark, its anger may make it attack the fishing boat as if it were a living enemy. Deep-sea fishing boats are usually too strong to be harmed by the

A diver wears a steel suit before mingling with a group of hungry sharks.

shark. But makos often leave some of their teeth in the boats.

Makos even have jumped right onto a boat deck and attacked the fisherman! They thrash around the deck, putting the fisherman in danger, until they surge back into the water. If the shark accidentally knocks the fisherman in the water, the fisherman can be in serious danger of being attacked.

The Shark Attack File

In 1958, a group of scientists formed the Shark Research Panel. They wanted to learn as much as they could about sharks. They also created the Shark Attack File. It contained reports and photographs of all known shark attacks. Most reports were not able to name the shark that attacked.

The Shark Attack File is no longer kept, but it revealed a lot about sharks.

Because sharks are made of cartilage, and not bone, nothing remains of them but their teeth.

Of the more than 370 types of sharks, only about 30 are dangerous to humans. Only three types of sharks account for most attacks. These are the great white, the tiger, and the bull shark.

About 20 makos attacked people while the Shark Attack File was kept. Usually, the people got in the way when a mako attacked a boat. Makos rarely swim in water shallow enough for swimmers, but they sometimes do so in Australia. There the swimmers must beware!

People are lucky that makos usually live so far out at sea. They are large, fast, and ferocious. If it liked shallow water, the mako shark might be even more dangerous than the great white!

Glossary

aggressive–full of energy; determined; willing to fight

ampullae of Lorenzini–fluid-filled sacs in sharks that can sense vibrations and help sharks "hear"

cartilage–a stiff but bendable body tissue. Sharks have a skeleton made of cartilage instead of bone.

claspers–a pair of organs located on the abdomen on a male shark, used for mating. They look like extra fins.

dorsal–located on the back of the shark, such as fins

gill slits–the long, straight openings on the side of a shark, into which water flows. A mako has five large gill slits.

keel–a flat part of the body that sticks out from another part, like the keel of a boat. A mako's keel strengthens its tail.

lateral line–a row of special sensory cells that is present along the side of a shark. It senses motion in the water

pectoral–located on the sides of the shark, such as fins

serrated–saw-toothed

species–a certain kind of animal or plant. Usually, creatures of one species only mate with each other.

streamlined–smooth-shaped for low resistance and fast movement through air or water

To Learn More

Blassingame, Wyatt. *Wonders of Sharks.* New York: Dodd, Mead, and Co., 1984.

Cerullo, Mary M. *Sharks: Challengers of the Deep.* New York: Cobblehill Books, 1993.

Freedman, Russel. *Sharks.* New York: Holiday House, 1985.

Langley, Andrew. *The World of Sharks.* New York: Bookwright Press, 1987.

Springer Victor G. and Joy P. Gould. *Sharks In Question: The Smithsonian Answer Book.* 1989.

Steel, Rodney. *Sharks of the World.* New York: Facts on File, 1989.

Sharks, Silent Hunters of the Deep. Readers Digest, 1987.

About the Author

Anne Welsbacher is publications director at the Science Museum of Minnesota. She writes science articles for various publications and is a playwright.

Index

ampullae of Lorenzini, 25-27, 43
ancient makos, 9
Atlantic Ocean, 16, 36
Australia, 4, 37, 42

bluefish, 23
bull sharks, 42

cartilage, 16, 43
cats, 25
claspers, 30, 43
coloring, 4, 9, 11

dolphins, 21

ears, 24
eggs, 29-30
eyes, 4, 25

fins, 4, 11, 16, 43-44
fishermen, 35, 38, 41

gill slits, 14-15, 43
great white sharks, 5, 15, 42
Gulf of Mexico, 36

herring, 23
hunting, 16, 19-24, 26-27, 33

keels, 11, 14-15, 44

lateral lines, 24, 43
leaping, 38
length, 5, 9, 29
longfin makos, 4, 16
lungs, 14

mackerel, 15, 20, 23
mackerel sharks, 15
Maori, 37
marlin, 21
mating, 29-30, 43

muscles, 15

New York, 36
New Zealand, 22, 37

oxygen, 14-15

Pacific Ocean, 16
porbeagles, 4

Puerto Rico, 38

range, 5, 16-17
scientific names, 4, 11
seals, 21
senses, 24-27, 43-44
Shark Attack File, 41-42
Shark Research Panel, 41
skeletons, 15, 43

skin, 11, 24
snouts, 7-8
speed, 7-9, 15, 23, 38
squid, 20, 23
swordfish, 21, 23-24

tails, 8, 11, 14-15, 37, 43
teeth, 4, 7, 9, 19-22, 33, 41
Texas, 36
tiger sharks, 42
tunas, 23

Virginia, 9

weight, 5, 9, 20-21
West Indies, 9